WHAT'S THAT I FEEL?

Adam Bellamy

Enslow Publishing
101 W. 23rd Street
Suite 240
New York, NY 10011
USA

enslow.com

Published in 2018 by Enslow Publishing, LLC.
101 W. 23rd Street, Suite 240, New York, NY 10011

Library of Congress Cataloguing-in-Publication Data

Names: Bellamy, Adam, author.
Title: What's that I feel? / Adam Bellamy.
Description: New York, NY : Enslow Publishing, 2018. | Series: All about my senses | Audience: Pre-K
  to grade 1. | Includes bibliographical references and index.
Identifiers: LCCN 2017002287| ISBN 9780766087200 (library-bound) | ISBN 9780766087996 (pbk.) |
ISBN 9780766088009 (6-pack)
Subjects: LCSH: Touch—Juvenile literature. | Senses and sensation—Juvenile literature.
Classification: LCC QP451 .B45 2018 | DDC 612.8/8—dc23
LC record available at https://lccn.loc.gov/2017002287

Printed in the United States of America

To Our Readers: We have done our best to make sure all websites in this book were active and appropriate when we went to press. However, the author and the publisher have no control over and assume no liability for the material available on those websites or on any websites they may link to. Any comments or suggestions can be sent by email to customerservice@enslow.com

Photo Credits: Cover, pg. 1 Clarissa Leahy/Taxi/Getty Images; pp. 3 (left), 12 Gorosi/Shutterstock.com; pp. 3 (center), 18 Beer1024/Shutterstock.com; pp. 3 (right), 20 Clover No.7 Photography/Moment Open/Getty Images; p. 4 Elena Masiutkina/Shutterstock.com; p. 6 Africa Studio/Shutterstock.com; p. 8 3445128471/Shutterstock.com; p. 10 PeopleImages/DigitalVision/Getty Images; p. 14 Thomas M Perkins/Shutterstock.com; p. 16 kali9/E+/Getty Images; p. 22 Madhavi108/Shutterstock.com.

Contents

Words to Know

prickly

rough

smooth

My sense of touch is very important. My skin helps me feel things. And my hands help me touch things.

My sense of touch helps me know when things are too hot.

My sense of touch also helps me feel when things are cold.

I can feel when things are soft, like a puppy's fur.

I can feel when things are prickly, like a pineapple.

I can feel when something tickles and makes me laugh!

And I can feel when something hurts. I feel pain when I fall.

When I touch something,
I can feel if it is rough.
The bark of a tree is hard
and rough.

I can feel if something is smooth. Many rocks at the beach are smooth.

I use my hands to touch and feel! It helps me learn about the world around me!

Read More

Issa, Joanna. *What Can I Feel?* Portsmouth, NH: Heinemann, 2014.

Murray, Julie. *I Can Touch*. Minneapolis, MN: Abdo Kids, 2015.

Wheeler-Toppen, Jodi Lyn. *Our Skin Can Touch*. North Mankato, MN: Capstone Press, 2017.

Websites

ABCYa.com
www.abcya.com/five_senses.htm
Fun cartoons help you learn about your senses.

Science for Kids
www.scienceforkidsclub.com/senses.html
Learn more about the senses.

Index

Guided Reading Level: C
Guided Reading Leveling System is based on the guidelines recommended by Fountas and Pinnell.

Word Count: 139